MEASURE

SHAKE

POUR

THE ELEMENTS OF
COCKTAIL MAKING

KURT MAITLAND

CIDER MILL
PRESS

BOOK
PUBLISHERS
KENNEBUNKPORT, MAINE

13-Digit ISBN: 978-1-60433-901-7
10-Digit ISBN: 1-60433-901-2

This book may be ordered by mail from the publisher. Please include $5.99 for
postage and handling. Please support your local bookseller first!

Books published by Cider Mill Press Book Publishers are available at special
discounts for bulk purchases in the United States by corporations, institutions, and
other organizations. For more information, please contact the publisher.

Cider Mill Press Book Publishers
"Where good books are ready for press"
PO Box 454
12 Spring Street
Kennebunkport, Maine 04046
Visit us online!
cidermillpress.com

Typography: Rival
All images used under official license from Shutterstock.com.

Printed in China
1 2 3 4 5 6 7 8 9 0
First Edition

CONTENTS

INTRODUCTION

THERE WAS A TIME, also known as the '80s and '90s, where the American landscape was quite the wasteland in terms of cocktails. There were a few faint glimmers of hope, such as barman Dale DeGroff, who became the polestar of New York nightlife while working behind the bar at the famed Rainbow Room.

But for the average person, one who wasn't a member of a club, didn't spend much time in hotel bars, or wasn't an aficionado, a cocktail was mainly of the Jack & Coke, Bloody Mary, Whiskey & Ginger, and Long Island Iced Tea variety.

Sure, these cocktails did the trick, i.e., got you tight*. But from the standpoint of flavor, and from the perspective of the cocktail renaissance we're living through today, one wouldn't even

---

*If you're unfamiliar with that term, put this book down, head to the closest used bookstore, and pick up a copy of *The Sun Also Rises*. It's great in its own right, and will also increase your enjoyment for the finer things in life, among which the intended products of this book are numbered.

bother to nurse a hangover with these antiquated concoctions.

Be glad those days are long gone.

The first sign that things were changing came when DeGroff's book, *The Craft of the Cocktail*, appeared in 2002. Containing drinks that were easy to make and a pleasure to drink, DeGroff's emphasis on fresh ingredients proved to be an invaluable lesson for myself and countless others. That book led me to my beloved Louis 649, a New York bar that, with its dark wood and continental emphasis on quality and atmosphere, was a world away from the libation-centric lounges I'd previously encountered. I was there frequently enough that I eventually made friends with the owner, Zach Sharaga, who provided me with a long string of drinks that proved quality ingredients and an inventive mind could do wonders with spirits.

I was so inspired by the cocktails Zach created while plying his craft that I decided to take a class with him at the bar, thinking it would, at the very least, provide a window into the alchemy he was practicing. The class was called "Cocktail 101—How to Mix Cocktails at Home," and we worked through a few basic cocktails— the Martini, Pimm's Cup, Daiquiri, Manhattan, and the Negroni.

What I will never forget is how emphatically Zach stressed the importance of ice. To me, ice was little more than frozen water, used to keep drinks cold. But Zach saw it as a crucial component of mixing cocktails, believing that utilizing bigger pieces of ice was guaranteed to produce better results than the convenient slivers issuing from the dispenser on your refrigerator. Today, with ice molds designed to produce large cubes and scintillating spheres readily available, this may not seem like a groundbreaking revelation. But for me, having spent all of my time in a bar on the patron side, it was eye-opening.

My intention is for this book to be a more in-depth version of that class. It may not be ice that provides the instant of illumination, but you'll come across a series of recommendations, tips, and techniques that will help you start to understand the level of craft required to fashion memorable cocktails. By memorable, I don't mean those drinks featuring 10 rare liquors, a bespoke mix, and a glamorous garnish, which you will find at some of the world's best bars. I mean learning what is required to turn out reliable, enjoyable versions of classics such as the Martini, Old Fashioned, and Tom Collins, which, with so few ingredients and so many ardent fans, are unforgiving of the slightest missteps.

To do that, you'll need to learn the strengths and weaknesses of the spirits you'll be using. Come to appreciate the importance of quality ice, and how flavoring a simple syrup is the easiest way to escalate a cocktail. Start to understand the different effects shaking and stirring will have on a drink, and become acquainted with a few other techniques employed by leading mixologists.

When done correctly, cocktails can make the good better and the excellent sublime. This book has everything you need to reach that rarefied air.

TOOLS OF
THE TRADE

YOU DON'T NEED TO purchase many things in order to start mixing cocktails, but there are some rudimentary supplies that are necessary if you want to try your hand at this game.

The following pages contain the must-haves for a basic home bar. Keep in mind that you don't have to break the bank to get started, but between glassware and bar tools, a little money will need to be spent. You can find basic bar and glassware sets on specialty sites like Cocktail Kingdom, as well as other online retailers. As with anything, the options will fit lots of budgets. If you are tight on funds, don't be deterred by used items. Soap and water come pretty cheap and you might find some real bargains on vintage gear to boot. Same goes for antique shops and yard sales. Hell, your parents might have some of the tools you need stashed away in a closet or basement. Nothing wrong with a little scavenging for a good cause.

JIGGER

A jigger is just a fancy name for the most common measuring tool in a bartender's arsenal, allowing you to quickly and easily measure "parts" or ounces. Most jiggers have a similar shape and capacity to a shot glass (about 1 to 1½ ounces).

MIXING GLASS

Nothing more than a tall glass in which to stir a drink. Typically a pint glass is used, but in a pinch, you can use any glass large enough to hold the necessary ingredients and a few ice cubes.

COCKTAIL SHAKER

A cocktail shaker provides a simple way to mix a cocktail, both combining the necessary ingredients, chilling them with ice, and diluting the cocktail slightly to remove any bite from the included spirits and allow their flavors to come to the fore. A basic cocktail shaker is relatively inexpensive, and you are better off purchasing this specific tool than trying to jury-rig a shaker for yourself.

The three-piece shaker, which is what you'll find in most homes, is known as the "Cobbler shaker." There are also two-piece shakers, consisting of two conical containers with flat bottoms, with one of the cones larger than the other. Known as a "Boston" or "French" shaker, these tend to be favored by professional bartenders because their "throw," the amount of space inside for the ingredients and ice to be combined, is greater than in the squatter Cobbler shaker. For more on the advantages and disadvantages of each, turn to the Mixing chapter.

HAWTHORNE STRAINER

 Used in tandem with either a mixing glass or a Boston shaker, the Hawthorne strainer simply strains the cocktail after it has been mixed.

The strainer's spring keeps the ice cubes (in the case of a mixing glass) or cubes and ice chips (in the case of a Boston shaker) out of a drink. Because the ice used to mix a cocktail has already started to melt, the strainer is an important tool for keeping a cocktail from becoming overly watered down.

You may also come across a Julep strainer as you start making your way into the world of mixology. This strainer, which was the predecessor to the Hawthorne, is a perforated, concave disk. It has fallen out of common use, but some bartenders prefer it when straining a cocktail containing small pieces of herb or a large amount of pulp.

PARING KNIFE

Chances are, there's already one in your kitchen, and it is essential for crafting the lemon-twist and lime-wedge garnishes that are a crucial part of numerous cocktails.

MUDDLER

Similar to a pestle, this simple tool is used to mash ("muddle") ingredients such as fruits or herbs. Muddling fruits releases the juice within, adding a fresh characteristic to a drink, while muddling certain herbs will help activate their  flavors. A simple muddler can often be found on the top end of a Cobbler shaker, though more refined muddlers are available for minimal cost.

BARSPOON

 There are numerous styles of barspoons, but most take the form of a spoon with a small bowl and a long, spiral shaft. Used in conjunction with a mixing glass, the purpose of the barspoon is to quickly and easily stir any cocktail. You can use any spoon—you just may find it more difficult to navigate the ice cubes. You will also come

across some recipes that call for a "barspoon" of a certain ingredient, which is equivalent to 1 teaspoon.

BLENDER

Essential for frozen drinks like the Piña Colada and Mudslide, a blender is also very handy for producing caster sugar (see page 74), or turning fruit into a puree that can add a velvety texture to a cocktail.

COCKTAIL GLASSES

The elegant promise of its thin stem and triangular bowl has become inseparable from the very idea of a cocktail, as evidenced by the name and its frequent inclusion on a bar's signage. It is typically utilized in cocktails that are served "up," such as the Martini.

HIGHBALL & COLLINS GLASSES

Highball and Collins glasses are tall and skinny and basically interchangeable, though Collins glasses are taller. Most commonly used in drinks that contain ice and a carbonated element such as club soda.

OLD FASHIONED GLASSES

Also known as rocks glasses, these are meant for spirits served "neat" and on the rocks. They are between 8 and 10 ounces; double Old Fashioned glasses are typically only a couple ounces larger and used for cocktails served over ice.

COUPES

The coupe has started to replace the traditional cocktail glass as the go-to for drinks that are served up, as its sleek curves lend an appealing refinement to a drink.

SHOT GLASSES

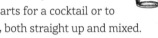

There is no standard size for a shot glass, but most land between 1¼ and 1½ ounces. They can be used to measure parts for a cocktail or to serve alcohol, both straight up and mixed.

CHAMPAGNE FLUTES

Sophisticated and celebratory, the thin bowl and delicate stem of a Champagne flute is a must for any sparkling cocktail.

THE SPIRIT
WORLD

NOW THAT YOU'VE ASSEMBLED your equipment, it's time to move on to the most important components: spirits. Since you are passionate enough about cocktails to purchase a book on the matter, I'm going to issue a commandment: don't go cut-rate on your spirits. As this is something that you want to enjoy, and use to provide others with enjoyment, working with subpar ingredients is counterproductive. The best you can get your hands on should be your focus when selecting liquor. Once you get the basics down, there are not many hard-and-fast rules in bartending, but steering clear of the bottom shelf at the liquor store is one.

With that settled, here are a few other rules of thumb that I've found helpful while building a home bar and my own craft:

1. If you are on a budget, discount vodka is more forgiving than cheap gin, whiskey, or tequila. Therefore, better to skimp on the vodka than the others.

2. Always remember that inexpensive is not

the same as cheap. For example, George Dickel and Old Overholt are inexpensive rye whiskies that lots of quality bars use to create an Old Fashioned. Can you get better ryes to work with? Yes. But, for certain cocktails, you don't have to.

3. Avoid store-bought flavored spirits (except in the case of vodka, where they can come in handy). If you want to add flavor to a specific liquor, you'll get far better results if you do the infusing yourself.

4. Keep an eye on your local spirits scene. You might find some great spirits that don't break the bank and offer inventive options that can make your cocktails unique.

VODKA

Vodka is the tofu of spirits. And though I'm not a huge fan of tofu, this comparison is meant to be a compliment, in that vodka's lack of a distinctive flavor allows it to find a comfortable place beside a stunning amount of other ingredients. I'm a fan of flavor in my drinks, be they wines, whiskies, or cocktails, so vodka's relative lack of flavor is a negative for me.

That said, vodka's lack of a strong flavor profile makes it a perfect spirit for cocktails. You can pair it with damn near anything, as evidenced by its presence in a diverse group of cocktails that spans from Martinis to Bloody Marys and White Russians. Vodka's versatility also means that you can literally add it to any type of fruit juice and voila . . . you have a cocktail—vodka and orange juice (a Screwdriver), vodka and cranberry juice (a Cape Cod), or vodka and grapefruit juice (a Greyhound). It plays well with many other spirits and complements whatever it is added to, which is not something you can say about other types of alcohol.

Vodka can be made from anything that can be fermented to create alcohol. This includes grains such as rye, barley, and wheat, as well as vegetables like beets and potatoes. The location of the distillery and what the distillers have the easiest access to will generally govern what is used to create vodka. Many countries use grain to make their vodka, with potatoes being a close second. Each imparts different advantages. Potato's high level of starch imparts a creamy, oily mouthfeel and a light, natural sweetness to vodka, while grains are thought to produce a cleaner spirit that is easier to work with.

GIN

Gin is also a clear spirit, but unlike vodka, it is not meant to "go gentle into that good night." If gin is in a cocktail, you'll know it. It's not necessarily the most difficult ingredient to work with (I think whiskey is harder); but its piney flavor just doesn't allow it to slink into the shadows the way that vodka can. Not to say that gin can't share the spotlight. Gin has the Martini crown locked down, and also adds its unique qualities to the Gin & Tonic (arguably the ultimate summer cocktail), the Negroni (the bartender's best friend), the Aviation, the Corpse Reviver No. 2, and the Bee's Knees, to name just a few cocktail cornerstones that rely on gin's inimitable flavor.

Today, many gins start with a neutral (flavorless)

alcohol and add botanicals afterward. Other producers elect to infuse their gin with essential oils, a method that allows for more affordable production, but is generally viewed as being less refined. Although the primary flavoring agent in gin will always be juniper, coriander, angelica, grains of paradise, cassia, orris root, caraway, and elderflower are other commonly used botanicals in the production of gin. And once Hendrick's, now one of the leading brands on the market, came out with a gin that had been infused with cucumber and rose, the world of gin became far more wide open. These unorthodox additions tempered the juniper just enough that the other flavors were able to enter the picture, and the overwhelming response Hendrick's received alerted other producers that gin may be far more malleable than previously believed. This realization has resulted in the wide range of gins available today, which includes those made from uncommon bases such as apple brandy and malt, and others that employ noncanonical botanicals such as mugwort and sarsaparilla.

Despite the excitement these innovative takes

have produced, the most popular style of gin remains London Dry, which refers to a gin that starts with a completely neutral base spirit before flavoring agents are added. In keeping with its name, a London Dry gin will typically be less sweet than other varieties, as well as higher in alcohol content. London Dry gin is also known for the inclusion of citrus peel among its botanicals, an element often detectable in its aroma.

Another good thing to keep in mind: gin has probably benefitted the most from the local distilling boom. Whether it be inventive flavoring options like spruce tips and chile peppers or barrel aging, these days most folks don't have to try too hard to find a great local gin that tastes better than the big-name options. It's certainly an excellent way to make your homemade versions of classic gin cocktails stand out, and to support your local artisans.

WHISKEY

No spirit appeals to the poet in us quite like whiskey. Immortalized in countless songs and literary works, the English writer George Bernard Shaw summed it up best when he said, "whisky is liquid sunshine." The sentiment swirling around the spirit is considerable, and very possibly spurred you to pick up this book. In reality, whiskey is the product of distillation and time. The distillation process starts with the creation of a "beer." This beer is different from what's on tap at your local, and is instead made from malted barley (Scotch), corn (bourbon), rye, wheat, or a combination of them all. The beer is brought to a boil and, since alcohol reaches its boiling point before water, that alcohol can be captured (as steam), collected, and condensed back into a liquid that will eventually become whiskey.

Whiskies are slippery, multifaceted beasts. Even within a distinct category—bourbon, for example—there are a variety of tastes and flavors to be had. Evan Williams Single Barrel and Four Roses are both bourbons, but they do not taste the same. There are bourbons that will burn your face off—George T. Stagg, a cask-strength release that often tops 120 proof, comes to mind—and there are others that you would happily sip in your backyard. And that's just one branch of the whiskey tree. Take a quick tour through Scotch, or Japanese whisky, and you will find yourself in a veritable forest of flavors.

That said, there are some characteristics that you'll want to be knowledgeable about when using the members of the whiskey family in cocktails. Bourbon, since it is made from corn, will be slightly sweet and typically features notes of caramel and vanilla, which you'll want to draw out further, or cut against to provide complexity.

Rye is dryer than bourbon, and typically features a peppery quality that goes well with citrus and the sweetness provided by many liqueurs.

Scotch, which is what most people think of the second they hear the word *whiskey* (even though it is called *whisky*, an alternative spelling utilized in Scotland, Japan, and other regions), is made and matured in Scotland using malted barley (whole grains of other cereals may be added). It must be aged in oak barrels for at least 3 years, and spirit caramel is allowed for color (unlike with bourbon).

Often, a cocktail recipe will call for Scotch as an ingredient. Fair enough, but that tells you nothing about what type of Scotch to use. Do you want a smoky single malt like an Ardbeg or a Laphroaig, or a sweeter one like a Balvenie? Or perhaps you would be wise to use a blend like Johnnie Walker instead? When this situation arises, you'd do well to take a brief gander at the drink's other ingredients: if they are sweet, you may want a Scotch with a bit of smoke in order to balance out that sweetness. Otherwise, you'll be pouring maple syrup on top of honey. Likewise, if the other ingredients are bitter or sour, a non-smoky Scotch may be your best option.

While this left-open-to-interpretation issue is most common in recipes featuring Scotch, I'd recommend a quick taste of any whiskey you are planning to mix in order to familiarize yourself with the flavors you'll be working with. When in doubt, taste.

TEQUILA

Tequila is a variety of mezcal, a group of liquors that are made by distilling the core of the agave plant, known as the *piña*. There are about 30 different varietals of agave plant that can be used to make mezcals, but only blue agave can be used for tequila.

When working with tequila, keep an eye out for mixtos, which are not 100 percent blue agave. These vitiated varieties are at the root of many of the unpleasant experiences that cause people to put tequila on their personal no-fly list, since there are more mixto brands on the market than pure agave brands. Legally, these mixto tequilas must be made with at least 51 percent pure blue agave sugar. The other half of the sugars can be from non-agave sources, like sugarcane, which will affect the taste and experience of the spirit in a negative fashion.

Pure tequila is known for its pleasant bite and the slightly mystical, energizing effect it can produce. As with most whiskey, tequila is aged in wooden barrels, and the amount of time spent in the barrel determines the character of the spirit that is bottled. Here's a brief overview of what you can expect from each:

- **Plata** is aged for no more than 2 months, and is also called blanco, silver, joven, or white tequila. Plata should taste fresh and fruity, with a clean, herbaceous hint. Its effortless embrace of lime juice makes it the go-to choice for a Margarita.

- **Reposado** spends 2 to 12 months in the barrel, and this longer stint allows the "rested" tequila to mellow out and acquire flavors ranging from oak to vanilla, baking spices, and fruit. It is used to add something new to classic tequila cocktails like the

Margarita, Paloma, and El Diablo, and can also stand in for bourbon or rye in treasured whiskey-based concoctions such as the Old Fashioned.

- **Añejo** refers to tequila that is aged between 1 and 3 years, providing it more depth and complexity than both plata and reposado, and a flavor that typically carries notes of wood, nuts, and chocolate. While each brand is unique in terms of wood used and resting time, all añejo tequila is going to be soft, smooth, and distinct on the palate.

- **Extra Añejo**, or "extra aged," will rest for at least 3 years before being bottled. It is a relative newcomer to the scene, only becoming an official classification in March 2006. The flavor will be similar to that of an añejo tequila, with certain aspects amplified per each distiller's preference.

RUM

Chances are, one of your first cocktails contained some form of rum, either the spicy Captain Morgan's that tends to go into a Rum & Coke, or the coconut-spiked Malibu that appears alongside a tropical juice in a number of entry-level drinks. But the recent tiki revival has brought white rum, aged rum, and black rum to the fore of the mixology world, proving that rum is a beast when it comes to crafting cocktails.

Rum is known for its sweetness, and, considering that it is made by distilling sugarcane or sugarcane by-products, there's no getting away from this aspect of its flavor profile. Rising from the sticky dregs of the sugar industry—which flourished in the Caribbean thanks to the free labor provided by slavery—the molasses that results from boiling the juice of harvested sugarcane was eventually fermented and distilled to create rum, and the spirit quickly became a sensation in the New World. So popular was rum in the American colonies that George Washington, running for the Virginia House of Burgesses in 1758, plied voters with the stuff.

From providing a counter to the mint in a Mojito or magnifying the creamy, coconuty goodness of a Piña Colada, white rum has a crisp, clear flavor that will cover most of your rum-related cocktail concerns. Dark rum gets its golden hue from barrel aging when it's done right, and from caramel coloring when done on the cheap, meaning the flavor of the latter won't be anywhere near as complex as the barrel-aged options. As with whiskey and tequila, the longer rum is aged, the more complex the flavor will be. Black rum, which is aged for much longer than white and dark rum, will be smokier than its fairer counterparts, and in possession of a flavor that is akin to a sweeter whiskey. Its subtlety and body can be a major boon amid the fruity mélanges that make up most tiki cocktails.

In your travels you may also come across rhum and caçhaca. The former is made from sugarcane juice instead of molasses, and, since it is not fermented before being distilled, it tends to be drier and more vegetal than its close cousin. Caçhaca is often referred to as "Brazilian rum," as it is the South American nation's preferred spirit. Like rum, it is fermented, but, as with rhum, sugarcane juice is the grist. This results in a grassier, rawer spirit that is more affected by elements like terroir and the type of wood used in the barrel than other rums.

OTHER SPIRITS

While the majority of your cocktail adventures will orbit around one of the preceding five spirits, particularly when you're starting out, you will come across many more liquors as you expand your horizons. A brief look at the most common and important of these follows.

Amaro: A group of bittersweet Italian herbal liqueurs that are usually consumed as an after-dinner digestif. Amaro come in a number of varieties, among which Cynar, Fernet-Branca, and Amaro Averna are the best known.

Aperol: A popular apéritif consisting primarily of gentian, rhubarb, and cinchona. It is similar in taste to Campari, but Aperol lacks Campari's bitterness and contains less than half of the alcohol.

Bénédictine: A popular French liqueur that contains 27 herbs and spices and is typically paired with brandy (a group of spirits resulting from the distillation of wine). The recipe for this sweet beverage is highly classified and rumored to be known to only three people at a given time.

Campari: An herbal, bitter apéritif that is best known for its misleading, candy apple red coloring and the crucial role it plays in a Negroni, where it manages to go toe-to-toe with the potent flavor of gin.

Cognac: Named for the French town it is made in, this is a variety of brandy produced by double-distilling very dry, acidic white wine and aging it in oak casks for at least 2 years, though many offerings will rest for longer than that. Its rich, sweet flavor and smooth finish make it a must for any home bar.

Curaçao: A liqueur flavored by the dried peel of the laraha citrus fruit (a descendant of the Seville orange) that is grown on the island that shares its name. Blue or orange food coloring is typically added to Curaçao to attain the exotic look it can lend to those cocktails that utilize it.

Domaine de Canton: A popular ginger liqueur that is made from a mixture of baby Vietnamese ginger, several varieties of Cognac, Tahitian vanilla, honey, and ginseng and renowned for its light-yet-strong flavor.

Lillet: An apéritif that is a blend of wines from France's Bordeaux region and citrus liqueurs. Typically served chilled, it is also part of the Vesper Martini, which Ian Fleming had James Bond order in the first 007 novel, *Casino Royale*.

Luxardo: A relatively dry liqueur that is produced through the distillation of the pits and sour fruit of the marasca cherry. It is commonly believed that it draws the best out of the other ingredients in a cocktail, particularly fruity components.

Mezcal: This relative of tequila has a smoky flavor that is a result of being cooked over charcoal in lava rock-lined pits that have been dug into the ground. With a production process that is heavily steeped in tradition, and a dizzying array of flavors available within the category, mezcal is increasingly being utilized and explored by the world's top mixologists.

Pimm's: A series of liqueurs that utilize different base alcohols. The most popular, Pimm's No. 1 Cup, is a gin-based digestif that has a reddish brown tint and hints of spice and citrus. It is frequently mixed with lemonade and garnished with slices of various fruits.

Pisco: A brandy that hails from winemaking regions in Peru and Chile. Best known as the base for the Pisco Sour cocktail, pisco is frequently substituted for gin in cocktails due to its heightened aromatic profile.

Sake: An alcoholic beverage made by fermenting rice that has been polished to remove the bran. The national drink of Japan, sake comes in a number of varieties, and is typically chilled before being consumed.

St-Germain: A sweet elderflower liqueur that is commonly paired with more straightforward spirits in order to provide complexity.

Vermouth: A fortified wine that has been infused with wormwood and various other herbs. Dry vermouth is white; sweet vermouth is red. As with any other spirit, the brand and quality matter. The French producers Dolin and Noilly Prat are trustworthy for dry vermouth, while Italian giants Cocchi and Carpano offer the most reliable sweet vermouth.

THE UNSUNG HEROES: ICE, SIMPLE SYRUP & BITTERS

THE LIQUOR AND YOUR mixing skills will receive most of the attention when you're bartending, but that doesn't mean you can afford to overlook these elements. Taking half-measures with any of them can take even top-shelf ingredients and flawless technique down a couple of pegs. Luckily, it's easy to avoid such pitfalls, and turn each member of this trio into an ally.

ICE

Everyone is familiar with ice as a substance. It cools down a drink and it makes the roads a nightmare in the winter. When it comes to cocktails, there are a few things you need to know. Ice is one of the most important aspects of a cocktail. It helps enhance the presentation, as few sights are more eye-catching than a frosted glass filled with clear, gleaming cubes and spheres, and it is an invaluable tool—either to cool down your drink as it is being shaken or stirred, or adding a little water to your creation in order to soften some of the harsher elements.

Just as low-quality spirits can spell doom

for a drink, bad ice can also sink a cocktail. Considering this, it's no surprise that some high-end bars have expensive machines to make blocks of clear, perfect ice; if you go on YouTube and look up Japanese bartenders and ice, you will see individuals wire-cutting a chunk of ice from an almost transparent block and then chipping away until they have a Platonic sphere that fits perfectly into a glass.

I'm going to make an assumption that most people reading this don't own a bar, aren't going to spend thousands of dollars on a machine that makes perfect ice, and don't have the time to hand-carve ice for each drink. But that doesn't mean you can't procure first-rate ice at home.

First off, use the best water you can get your hands on. This is pretty straightforward. The better the water, the better the ice. Filtering what comes out of your tap is a must. Spring or distilled water are worthy of consideration. If crystal-clear ice is of the utmost importance, you'll want to use distilled water, boil it twice, and let it cool completely before adding it to the ice-cube trays. Distilling the water removes most of the air and minerals from it, which are the elements that make for cloudy ice. Boiling it will extract whatever air and minerals remain, and the care taken with the resulting cubes will be transparent to all.

Once you've sorted out the water, you need something that can provide the desired form. Standard plastic ice-cube trays can work in a pinch, but you *may* (hint, hint) want to make a small investment in some silicone trays that produce larger cubes and spheres. The increased surface area will cause the ice to melt slower, helping you avoid the dreaded "watery drink" phenomenon.

Another thing to remember: ice trays take on the smells of the freezer (though metal trays do not hold onto odors as much as plastic and silicone trays). Since no one wants ice that smells like a batch of stew, I suggest the following:

- Wash your ice trays before a big party— soap and water should be fine with regular trays; soap, water, and baking soda is the move with silicone trays because even though they make amazing ice, the silicone picks up more odors than a standard tray. In fact, giving the freezer a good scrub before making ice for the big party wouldn't hurt.

- Have a set of trays that is only used for cocktail ice—ice trays can't pick up freezer smells if they aren't in the freezer all of the time. Keep this set in freezer bags in a kitchen cabinet (though be sure to keep them away from the oven and stove since cooking will impart odors as well) to reduce the aromas your ice cubes pick up.

- Make fresh ice for each party—the best way to avoid stinky, stale ice is to minimize the time the ice is in the freezer, meaning you'd be wise to make fresh batches the day of or the day before the party.

- If you need to make crushed ice, don't rely on the refrigerator dispenser. Rather, get a Lewis bag and mallet. Back in the nineteenth century, these canvas sacks were a staple in bars. Just add some of your freshly made cubes to the bag, give it a couple of whacks, and, voila, you have homemade crushed ice that is perfect for cocktails, as well as a nice stress reliever.

SIMPLE SYRUP

Named due to its humble components—equal parts sugar and water—and the ease of making it—just place the sugar and water in a saucepan, stir as it comes to a boil in order to help the sugar dissolve, and then let it cool—there is nothing basic about the role simple syrup plays in cocktail making.

Whether it is there to offset the lemon or lime juice, allow a tucked-away flavor to surface, or add body and viscosity to a drink, the syrup produced in the following preparation definitively transcends its modest construction.

INGREDIENTS
1 cup water
1 cup granulated sugar

Place the ingredients in a medium saucepan and bring to a boil, while stirring to help the sugar dissolve. When the sugar has dissolved, remove the pan from heat and let the syrup cool before using. The syrup will keep in a tightly sealed container in the refrigerator for up to 1 month.

OTHER HELPFUL SYRUPS

Simple syrup will keep you in good stead for the majority of the cocktails you encounter, but there are some drinks that require a little more in the syrup department. When you encounter one of these instances, or if you're looking for some way to make a cocktail all your own, give one of the following syrups a try.

Orgeat: This rich French syrup is the key component in a number of tropical drinks, such as the Mai Tai. To make orgeat, preheat the oven to 400°F. Place 2 cups almonds on a baking sheet and toast in the oven for 5 minutes. Remove and let cool. Once cool, place the nuts in a food processor or blender and pulse until they have been crushed into a coarse meal. Place 1 cup of simple syrup in a saucepan and warm it over medium heat. Add the almond meal, remove the pan from heat, and let the mixture stand for 3 to 6 hours. Strain the mixture through cheesecloth and discard the solids. Add 1 teaspoon of orange blossom water and 2 oz. vodka and stir to combine.

Grenadine: A red, nonalcoholic syrup that is used to add sweetness and/or color to a cocktail, grenadine is now commonly produced using artificial ingredients. If you'd like to bring it back to its roots, place 2 cups of 100 percent pomegranate juice in a saucepan and bring to a simmer over medium-low heat. Simmer until reduced by half, add 1 cup of sugar, and stir until all of the sugar has dissolved. Remove from heat, let cool before using, and store in the refrigerator for up to 1 month.

Vanilla Syrup: Use vanilla syrup to provide balance in a drink that has an extremely sour or smoky component. To make vanilla syrup, add 2 split vanilla beans or 1 oz. pure vanilla extract to a standard simple syrup after the sugar has dissolved. Remove from heat, let cool, and strain if using vanilla beans.

Herbal Syrup: As with anything cocktail-related, you'll want to adjust the amount to suit your own taste, but a good general recipe is 4 sprigs of woody herbs like rosemary or thyme, and 10 leaves from soft herbs such as basil, mint, or cilantro. Add the chosen herb to a standard simple syrup after the sugar has dissolved. Remove from heat, let cool, and strain before using. Refrain from using ground or dried herbs when flavoring a syrup, as these will be difficult to remove and will lend your cocktail a grainy, unpleasant mouthfeel.

Cinnamon Syrup: Cinnamon's unparalleled combination of sweet and spice makes it a wonderful addition to a number of cocktails featuring brown spirits like whiskey, tequila, and dark rum. To make cinnamon syrup, add 3 cinnamon sticks to a standard simple syrup after the sugar has dissolved. Remove from heat, let stand until cool, and remove the cinnamon sticks before storing in the refrigerator.

Tea-Infused Syrup: Adding the smoky nature of Lapsang souchong, Earl Grey's unique citrusy quality, or the softness of chamomile to a simple syrup is another great way to put your own stamp on a cocktail. To make a tea-based syrup, add 3 tea bags or 3 teaspoons of loose-leaf tea to a standard simple syrup after the sugar has dissolved. Remove from heat, let stand until cool, and strain before using.

BITTERS

The recent cocktail renaissance has lifted bitters from a small village where Angostura and Peychaud's were the only inhabitants to a metropolis filled with bespoke alloys and individuals who treat these mysterious tonics with special reverence.

This level of devotion may seem like a bit much, but, considering where bitters originated, it is actually quite fitting. Bitters were initially curatives produced by the European monks that were charged with treating illness before medicine was established as a field. They created their remedies out of herbs, roots, barks, flowers, and spices, creating a series of potions that proved effective enough to be handed down through the centuries. When apothecaries took over the task of providing the public with nostrums, an extremely interesting discovery was made by those who mixed bitters with liquor in order to get the medicine to go down easier: the bitters also worked as a salve for the spirits, taking the bite out of the booze and highlighting its toothsome qualities.

It should come as no surprise, then, that the stalwarts of the bitters world, Angostura and Peychaud's, were both the work of medicine men. Angostura, which Johann G. B. Siegert created while serving as Simón Bolívar's surgeon general, contains over 40 ingredients, though the actual recipe is known by only five people on Earth at any time, and those five take their duty so seriously that they have agreed to never fly on a plane together, knowing that the formula for Angostura would be lost forever in the event of a crash.

Peychaud's was created by a New Orleans pharmacist named Antoine Amedee Peychaud, who liked the effect his family's bitters recipe had on various spirits. Peychaud sold his bitters around town, and when the Merchant's Exchange House mixed them with Cognac and absinthe, the resulting drink, the Sazerac, was such a hit that by the 1890s it was being bottled and sold around the US.

The role of Angostura and Peychaud's in the cocktail world is similar to the one salt plays in food—a small amount provides balance and accentuates each element so that its full weight can be felt. When adding bitters to a cocktail, act as you would while adding something spicy or pungent to a dish, remaining mindful that you can always add more, but it's impossible to remove once it's in there.

As drinks become more complex and feature increasingly unorthodox ingredients, mixologists have started to explore the long-neglected world of bitters in search of tinctures that go beyond what Angostura and Peychaud's offer. If you're interested in seeing what else is out there, give the offerings from Fee Brothers, Bittermens, Dr. Adam Elmegirab, and Bittercube a look.

MIXING

WHERE THE RUBBER MEETS the road. It's nice to have outfitted yourself with all of the required kit and maintained a fanatical devotion to high-quality ingredients, but if you don't know how to utilize them properly, all that careful preparation and passion ends up not mattering much.

Luckily, there aren't too many moving parts when it comes to mixing cocktails. Consistently excellent results are accessible if one adheres to a few fundamentals.

To start, always add the ingredients to the cocktail shaker or mixing glass before adding the ice.

When you do add ice, the more, the merrier. If you don't use enough ice, it will melt in the mixing vessel and you'll be left with a drink that is too watery for anyone's liking. A good rule of thumb is to fill the cocktail shaker or mixing glass about two-thirds of the way with ice. It's also imperative that you use full cubes instead of crushed ice to avoid overdiluting the cocktail. Another good thing to keep in mind: the larger the surface area of the ice, the longer you will have to shake or stir the cocktail to properly chill, combine, and dilute it.

As for whether to use a cocktail shaker or a mixing glass to combine the cocktail, you want to take the ingredients and the cocktail's desired effect into account. Drinks containing juice, dairy, or egg white should be shaken, as the additional force will aerate the cocktail and create a thick, velvety froth that is as pleasing to the eye as it is to the tongue.

Drinks that are comprised only of spirits (unless one of them is a cream liqueur, such as Baileys) should be stirred, since you are not after froth, but a smooth and strong consistency featuring minimal dilution. Some believe that shaking a cocktail which does not have an aerating element to cushion it will "bruise" the liquor, lending it a bitterness that is sure to stand out amid the delicate play of flavors in a mixed drink.

Cocktails that contain a carbonated element such as club soda should be stirred, since shaking it will remove all of the carbonation. This is such a concern that it is recommended you add the fizzy component to the cocktail after it has been strained into the glass, and then stir gently so as to just intermingle it with the other ingredients.

Now, as some probably wondered upon encountering the "stir spirits-only cocktails" maxim, to the age-old debate that the fictional James Bond ignited when he insisted that his Martini be "shaken, not stirred."

The argument has been granted such weight that even scientists have entered the fray, conducting studies, performing research, and identifying empirical, quantifiable differences between the shaken and stirred Martini.

John Hayes, a food science professor at Penn State University, once told NPR that shaking a Martini dilutes the drink, giving it a more watery quality. Unlike stirring, shaking a cocktail chips away at the ice, resulting in tiny flakes that melt as the drink warms. On the other hand, these tiny ice flakes help keep the drink cold for a longer period of time.

Bartender Darcy O'Neil, operating on the popular theory that Bond's preference was attributable to shaking being a better option for incorporating the oily quality of a potato vodka, performed tests which confirm that shaking a Martini made with potato vodka successfully dissipates that oil. He also agrees that shaking a Martini will make it colder, but notes that after 20 shakes or so, a cocktail has generally gotten as cold as it's going to get.

Boston-based culinary scientist Dave Arnold agrees with O'Neil that shaking a cocktail will make it colder, but points out that the ability to detect certain flavors is impeded when a drink becomes too cold. Sweetness, in particular, becomes more difficult to taste, and Arnold recommends adding a dash of simple syrup if you plan to shake a traditionally stirred cocktail.

So, what's the verdict?

Those in search of a traditional experience should

stir a spirits-only drink such as the Martini. Those who want to ensure that the ingredients are combined as thoroughly as possible should try shaking their drink. Those looking for a colder drink should shake it. Those who desire a sweeter drink should stir it. In the end, the two methods produce different results, but which version is "better" is ultimately determined by personal preference.

While stirring will produce a cocktail that is less cold than shaking it will, you still want the cocktail to be cold. This will take much longer with a mixing glass than with a shaker, around two to three times as long. To do this, add the ingredients to the mixing glass, fill it two-thirds of the way with ice, and then, working in a circular motion rather than up and down, use a barspoon to stir the drink.

When it comes to shaking, it is up to you whether you want a Boston shaker or a Cobbler shaker to be your primary implement. Both have their advantages and disadvantages. The Boston shaker grants the ingredients and ice more space to be mixed in and allows them to emulsify better. The Cobbler shaker is easier to use, and some bartenders believe it makes it easier to control the ice in the shaker, keeping it away from the bottom and preventing too many small chips from entering a drink.

If using a Boston shaker, place the ingredients in the smaller container, fill the larger container two-thirds of the way with ice, quickly invert it over the container with the ingredients, taking care not to spill any ice, and then create a seal between the two containers. Hold each container with one hand and shake vigorously for about 12 seconds to properly chill and combine the ingredients. Gently tap the seal while holding onto the larger container in order to uncouple the pieces, place a Hawthorne strainer over the top of the container containing the drink, and strain the cocktail into the selected glass.

If using a Cobbler shaker, add the ingredients and fill it two-thirds of the way with ice. Secure the top and the cap and then shake vigorously for 15 seconds. The slightly longer shaking time is necessary due to the reduced volume of the Cobbler shaker. After 15 seconds, remove the cap and hold the shaker by the top as you strain the drink into the glass.

These techniques will suit almost every cocktail, but the following are a few specialized methods which top-flight bartenders will employ if the occasion calls for it.

Cuban roll: Residing in the space between stirring and shaking (offering more dilution and texture than the former while being gentler than the latter), this method consists of pouring the ingredients and ice between two containers until they are chilled and combined.

Double-strain: When the mixing vessel contains pulp or herbs, the strainer may not remove everything, meaning the clean mouthfeel you're after could be imperiled. To avoid that issue, place a fine-mesh strainer over the mouth of the glass and strain the cocktail through this.

Dry shake: Egg white provides cocktails with

a beautiful and delectable foam, but it can be difficult to incorporate due to its viscous nature. To combat this issue and ensure that the egg white is emulsified, many bartenders will shake the ingredients without any ice before adding ice and shaking the cocktail to chill it. Some bartenders will even place the spring from a Hawthorne strainer in the shaker while dry shaking, believing that it acts as a whisk. In recent years, the reverse dry shake—straining a shaken cocktail, discarding the ice, returning the cocktail to the shaker, and shaking it again—has gained favor, as it is believed to produce a more robust foam. But there are some who feel the reverse dry shake has gained momentum due primarily to the rise of social media, as it creates a foam that looks better, but is lacking in texture.

Swizzle method: Used to combine cocktails featuring crushed ice, the swizzle method will quickly chill and aerate a drink. Some bartenders believe that this method does a better job of drawing out aromas than shaking or stirring. To mix a cocktail using the swizzle method, place a swizzle stick between your hands, lower the swizzle stick into the drink, and quickly rub your palms together to rotate the stick as you move it up and down in the drink. When frost begins to form on the outside of the vessel, the cocktail is ready to be enjoyed.

Whip shake: This method utilizes two hands and a very small amount of ice (one or two cubes) to shake a cocktail as hard as possible in a short period of time, resulting in a cocktail with an exceptionally creamy consistency.

WHAT WE TALK ABOUT WHEN
WE TALK ABOUT COCKTAILS

The instructions that are occasionally appended to a cocktail order can be the source of considerable confusion. If someone asks for a cocktail "straight up," that means it should be served in the proper glass, with no ice. If someone asks for a drink "up," it usually means that they are looking for a cocktail that is typically served over ice—or "on the rocks"—to be strained into a cocktail glass or coupe, with no ice. But you could also ask for a shot of liquor to be served up, which means that you are looking for it to be chilled and diluted in a cocktail shaker before being strained into a glass. "Neat" refers to a shot of liquor poured directly from the bottle to glass, with no chilling or diluting involved.

THE CLASSICS

INNOVATION IS WONDERFUL, BUT almost everyone who happens past your home bar is going to ask for one of the following standards. And, chances are, they are attached enough to their request that their opinion of your bartending, and their willingness to drop by in the future, depends on how you handle their beloved tipple. Considering that, plus the fact that these cocktails are still beguiling the world's best bartenders, a good deal of what you end up learning about the craft of cocktail making will be through your experiences with these touchstones.

MARTINI

A cocktail that has weathered every shift in fashion and managed to retain its place as the epitome of refinement. A drink that, working with just two ingredients, is able to astound seasoned aficionados and dazzle the uninitiated. Easy to make and difficult to master, revered for its simplicity and adaptability, the Martini is a cocktail one could spend a life with, as noted by American historian Bernard DeVoto, who once said, "It is one of the happiest marriages on earth, and one of the shortest lived."

INGREDIENTS

3 oz. gin

½ oz. dry vermouth

1 lemon twist or green olives, for garnish

Place a cocktail glass in the freezer. Add the gin and vermouth to a mixing glass and then fill it two-thirds of the way with ice. Stir with a barspoon until the glass starts to frost, about 20 seconds. Remove the cocktail glass from the freezer, strain the cocktail into the glass, and garnish with a lemon twist or a few green olives.

WHAT'S THE SECRET?

Working with a quality vermouth. It is a small, and frequently maligned, part of the Martini, but assuming this is an indication that it is unimportant will take you far afield. The dry vermouth from Dolin and Noilly Prat each has a long history of serving Martini fans well. Once you incorporate that lesson, the Martini is an exercise in restraint. It can be tempting to add more gin to the mix, or to toss the ingredients into a shaker since cold seems to be key, but it is imperative that you take your cue from the drink itself, and remember to always keep it simple.

THE GREAT DIVIDE

I am among those who do not consider a vodka Martini to be a "true" Martini, but there is no denying that the vodka Martini has accrued a passionate following of its own, with many following James Bond's example and settling into the familiar, comforting arms of vodka.

While I hesitate to brand it a Martini, the truth is that the vodka Martini is no less elegant, no less flavorful, and no less perfect a cocktail than its gin counterpart. It simply makes use of a different primary ingredient, one which has different strengths and weaknesses. And, by not forcing the other ingredients to stand up to a bold flavor like juniper, vodka greatly expands your options when it comes to fun and whimsical takes on a Martini.

In the end, I believe that even the most ardent of gin lovers would do well to sample a vodka Martini. They may find that they prefer to remain loyal to the gin-centric classic. That's perfectly fine. Or they may find an entirely new reason to love the Martini.

OLD FASHIONED

As James Bond embedded the Martini in the public consciousness, the Old Fashioned owes its current popularity to a figment of someone's imagination. As the go-to drink for the stylish, and extremely thirsty, Don Draper on the lauded TV show *Mad Men*, the Old Fashioned lost the extraneous elements—club soda is just one—that had been appended to it over the years, returned to its roots, and became the quintessential whiskey cocktail.

INGREDIENTS

1 teaspoon caster sugar
2 to 3 dashes of bitters
Dash of water
2 oz. bourbon or rye whiskey
1 strip of lemon zest, for garnish
1 Luxardo maraschino cherry, for garnish

Place the sugar, bitters, and water in a double Old Fashioned glass and stir until the sugar has dissolved. Fill the glass with ice, add the whiskey, and stir until chilled. Express the strip of lemon zest over the cocktail, drop it into the glass, and finish with the Luxardo maraschino cherry.

WHAT'S THE SECRET?

Exploring the space within the drink's narrow parameters in order to find something all your own. Try out different bitters, or use a mixture, such as a few drops of Angostura and Regan's Orange. Remove the cherry and instead add a bit of the juice from a jar of Luxardo maraschino cherries or griottines (cherries steeped in kirsch, a cherry brandy) before adding the whiskey. Add the strip of lemon zest with the sugar and muddle it, or switch it out for a piece of orange zest. When you really start to drill down into the elements of this simple cocktail, the possibilities are endless. You could also just strip the cocktail down to its primordial form: sugar, bitters, and whiskey, as some believe that everything else was added to ease the sting of the dubious spirits that circulated during Prohibition.

DO NOT CAST IT ASIDE

Caster sugar is a super-fine sugar with a consistency that sits somewhere between granulated sugar and confectioners' sugar. Since it can dissolve without heat, unlike granulated sugar, it is tailor-made for cocktails. This ideal fit comes with a hefty price tag at the store, but you can easily make caster sugar at home with nothing more than a food processor or a blender and some granulated sugar. Place the granulated sugar in the food processor or blender and pulse until the consistency is super-fine, but short of powdery. Let the sugar settle in the food processor, transfer it to a container, and label to avoid future confusion.

MINT JULEP

This drink is permanently associated with Kentucky, both due to the Kentucky Derby, where it became the official beverage in 1938, and because of the bourbon that the state is renowned for producing. This is the version preferred by legendary Kentucky senator Henry Clay, who helped popularize the cocktail when he brought it to D.C. in the nineteenth century.

INGREDIENTS

12 fresh mint leaves
1 barspoon of granulated sugar
2 oz. bourbon
Water, to top
Seltzer water, to top
1 sprig of mint, for garnish
1 strip of lemon zest, for garnish
Confectioners' sugar, for garnish

Slap the mint leaves and rub them around the inside of a chilled tin Julep cup (or a double Old Fashioned glass). Place them in the glass, add the granulated sugar and a dash of the bourbon, and muddle. Fill the glass with crushed ice, add the remaining bourbon, and then fill the rest of the glass with equal parts water and seltzer water. Place the sprig of mint on top, express the strip of lemon zest over the cocktail and add it as a twist, and dust with confectioners' sugar.

WHAT'S THE SECRET?

Doing all you can to extract as much of the mint's aroma as possible, since the Julep is a drink that is meant to charm the nose as much as the taste buds. Also, you want to be extremely careful in your handling of the tin Julep cup, as it will lose some of the precious cold with every touch of a finger. And, if you still struggle to get a handle on it, try stirring the cocktail after adding the bourbon. It's not traditional, as purists feel the additional agitation will dilute the cocktail too much, but it just may add an element that you or someone else will find extremely pleasing.

EXPRESS YOURSELF

Expressing a strip of citrus zest simply means twisting it into a tight spiral over a cocktail in order to impart the oils into the drink, adding considerable flavor and aroma. The zest can then be added to the cocktail as a garnish or discarded.

MARGARITA

Sometimes three is not a crowd, but the magic number. This perfect marriage of tequila, orange liqueur, and lime juice is a riff on the Daisy, a cocktail that was popular during the '30s and '40s. The connection becomes clear when one realizes that *margarita* is the Spanish word for "daisy." While much debate rages over who came up with the cocktail, its pleasant taste and unquestioned status as the signal that it's time to let the good times roll has made it the most popular cocktail in America.

INGREDIENTS

1 lime wheel
Salt, to taste
2 oz. silver tequila
1 oz. triple sec
1 oz. fresh lime juice

Generously rub the rim of your chosen glassware with the lime wheel, set the lime wheel aside, and then dip the glass's rim into the salt. Place the tequila, triple sec, and lime juice in a cocktail shaker, fill it two-thirds of the way with ice, and then shake vigorously until chilled and combined. If desired, add ice to the rimmed glass. Strain the cocktail into the glass and use the lime wheel as a garnish.

WHAT'S THE SECRET?

Avoiding the less-pure mixtos that make people squeamish about tequila is essential. If the famed bite of silver tequila isn't quite to your liking, try the more mellow reposado, which cools out a bit thanks to more time in the barrel. If you or a guest is a fan of whiskey—Scotch in particular—consider utilizing mezcal as the base. Swapping some of the triple sec out for some simple syrup or agave nectar also has a healthy number of fans, and is worth investigating if the blessed trinity—silver tequila, triple sec, and fresh lime juice—leaves you wanting a little more.

SO FRESH AND SO CLEAN

Not every recipe you come across will specify, but you're going to want to make sure you use fresh lime and lemon juice any time they are included as ingredients in a cocktail recipe. The store-bought varieties can include chemicals that will take your concoctions wide of the mark if you toss them into the shaker. It will also be helpful to know how much juice a lemon and lime contain so that you can prepare properly before the party. On average, a lemon and a lime will each have 2 tablespoons, or 1 ounce, of juice.

DAIQUIRI

A world away from the packaged, cloyingly sweet slush that many people know from the restaurant excursions of their youth and trips to the tropics. The classic version is simple and crisp, and its perfect balance of tart and sweet is beloved by bartenders everywhere. Retire to a shady spot with one of these on a hot summer day and you'll see why those who know turn to the Daiquiri time and again.

INGREDIENTS

2 oz. white rum
½ oz. fresh lime juice
½ teaspoon caster sugar
1 lime wheel, for garnish

Place a coupe in the freezer 5 minutes before you are going to prepare the cocktail. Add the rum, lime juice, and caster sugar to a cocktail shaker, fill it two-thirds of the way with ice, and shake vigorously until chilled and combined. Remove the coupe from the freezer, strain the cocktail into it, and garnish with the lime wheel.

WHAT'S THE SECRET?

Refraining from venturing into too-sweet territory. You want to use just enough caster sugar to take the edge off of the lime juice, so that the cocktail can fulfill its potential as a refreshing tonic. Some leading bartenders also suggest using half crushed and half cubed ice in the shaker, believing that the additional dilution allows the drink to land in the ideal spot between sweet and sour.

OUR FATHER

Ernest Hemingway's impact on literature was immense, but it could be argued that his influence on cocktail culture was even larger. Featuring prominently in the history of the Bloody Mary, the Martini, and the Mojito, Hemingway also lends his name to the most popular variation on the Daiquiri.

It would be reasonable to assume that this twist is exactly what Hemingway quaffed at one of his favorite watering holes, Havana's famed El Floridita, where Papa enjoyed his Daiquiris with shaved ice, a splash of lime juice, twice the typical amount of rum, and no sugar, on account of his diabetes. But since that is a higher-octane concoction than most could handle, the El Floridita appended its famous patron's name to a far friendlier iteration that features 2 oz. white rum, ¾ oz. fresh grapefruit juice, ½ oz. fresh lime juice, ¼ oz. Luxardo, ¼ oz. simple syrup, and a grapefruit twist for garnish. Tart with a subtle sweetness, the Hemingway Daiquiri is, like its inspiration, vigorous, to the point, and capable of surprising depth.

TOM COLLINS

One of history's most enduring cocktails, this archetypical highball was traditionally made using Old Tom gin, but when the citrus-forward flavor of London Dry took a stranglehold on the market, the sweeter Old Tom was pushed to the brink of extinction. The revival of classic cocktails has brought Old Tom back, and I highly recommend trying the drink as it was intended. After all, it worked well enough to carry the Collins all the way from the early nineteenth century to the present.

INGREDIENTS

2 oz. Old Tom or London Dry gin

1 oz. simple syrup, or to taste

¾ oz. fresh lemon juice

Club soda, to top

1 lemon wheel, for garnish

1 Luxardo maraschino cherry, for garnish

Place the gin, simple syrup, and lemon juice in a cocktail shaker and then fill it two-thirds of the way with ice. Shake until chilled and combined and strain it into a chilled Collins glass that is full of ice. Top with the club soda and garnish with the lemon wheel and cherry.

WHAT'S THE SECRET?

For starters, the simple syrup. The amount required may change depending on which gin you use, so remain mindful of that when mixing. Also, don't be afraid to increase the amount of lemon juice if this recipe results in a drink that is just not quite as refreshing as it seems it should be. There's a lot of space for tweaking between all those bubbles, and playing with the amount of sweet and tart is how you bring this drink to its breezy apex. You also want the Collins, and any fizz, to be as cold and undiluted as possible. Chilling the Collins glass is a good start, but filling it with as much ice as you can is another way to guarantee a satisfactory result.

MOJITO

While the presence of rum, lime, and sugar means that Havana, the Cuban capital, flows through the veins of this cocktail, it is rumored that its name is derived from the West African word *mojo*, which means "to cast a little spell." When the search for a fitting moniker casts that wide of a net, you can be certain you're dealing with something special. And, as advertised, the refreshing character of a well-made Mojito is certain to put everyone who encounters it in a pleasant daze.

MEASURE, SHAKE, POUR

INGREDIENTS

8 to 10 fresh mint leaves

1 oz. simple syrup

1 oz. fresh lime juice

2 oz. white rum

1 sprig of mint, for garnish

Place the mint leaves in the palm of one hand and slap them to activate their aroma. Place them in the bottom of a Collins glass and add the simple syrup and lime juice. Fill the glass halfway with crushed ice. Gently stir until lightly chilled, about 10 seconds. Add the rum and more crushed ice and briefly stir to combine. Fill the remainder of the glass with crushed ice and garnish with the sprig of mint.

WHAT'S THE SECRET?

Not adding too much simple syrup, and leaning toward the dryer end of the spectrum when selecting a rum. Brugal Especial Extra Dry, a blend of aged rums that is produced in the Dominican Republic, is a quality and very affordable dry rum. The drink should also be extremely cold, otherwise the strong flavor of mint will push everything else aside. Many will put club soda in a Mojito nowadays, but I think that the effervescence it provides is not worth washing away the complexity provided by the combination of rum, lime juice, and mint.

BLOODY MARY

As those who have mastered this particular recipe are all too aware, this cocktail is too good to be restricted to brunch, where its glory is threatened by long waits and mediocre, overpriced eggs. Refreshing, invigorating, and able to facilitate any number of innovations, it's just a matter of time before this becomes a go-to morning, noon, and night.

INGREDIENTS

1 tablespoon fresh lemon juice

1 tablespoon fresh lime juice

4 oz. tomato juice

2 dashes of Worcestershire sauce

Pinch of sea salt

Pinch of celery salt

Pinch of coarsely ground black pepper

¼ teaspoon peeled and
grated horseradish

2 oz. vodka

1 green olive, for garnish

1 celery stalk, for garnish

Place all of the cocktail ingredients in a cocktail shaker filled two-thirds of the way with ice and shake vigorously until chilled and combined. Strain into a pint glass or a Collins glass filled with ice and garnish with the green olive and the celery stalk.

WHAT'S THE SECRET?

Keep close tabs on the celery salt and Worcestershire sauce. A heavy hand with either of these ingredients will have people wondering if you added actual blood to the drink. The Bloody Mary is also a good time to utilize the Cuban roll method (see page 61) for mixing cocktails, as the slightly gentler approach allows the tomato juice to retain its thickness, granting the final cocktail a velvety quality that will be hugely appreciated. If you have time, it's worth giving this a try: place all of the ingredients, except for the vodka and garnishes, in a cocktail shaker, stir to combine, cover, and store in the refrigerator overnight, giving the flavor plenty of time to develop before adding the vodka and mixing the cocktail.

A SERENDIPITOUS STALK

The celery stalk has become such an integral part of the Bloody Mary that, at this point, it is fair to call them a married couple. You wouldn't think it, but this pale green vegetable has a long history as a curative, with its medicinal use noted as far back as Homer's *Odyssey*. Knowing that it has long been used to treat colds, the flu, digestive ailments, and issues with water retention, it makes perfect sense that someone looking to take the edge off their hangover with a Bloody Mary would add a celery stalk as an additional restorative. But this happy union appears to have occurred entirely by accident. Legend has it that in the early 1960s, a customer at Chicago's Pump Room (the beloved restaurant closed in 2017) couldn't wait for his server to bring him a swizzle stick for his Bloody Mary. Taking matters into his own hands, he snatched a celery stalk from a nearby tray and was smitten by the element it added to the drink. Just like that, the celery-stalk garnish became essential, clearing the palate and providing much-needed hydration after a long night.

NEGRONI

A favorite of luminaries such as Ernest Hemingway, Orson Welles, and Anthony Bourdain and long treasured by bartenders everywhere, the Negroni currently carries as much clout as any classic cocktail. Thanks to its deep, appealing red coloring and the incomparable fusion of bitter, sweet, and woodsy flavors, you won't regret jumping on this bandwagon. As Kingsley Amis, the great English author and spirits aficionado (his *On Drink* is highly recommended, both for the humor and helpful tips), once said of the Negroni, "It has the power, rare with drinks and indeed with anything else, of cheering you up."

INGREDIENTS

1 oz. Campari

1 oz. sweet vermouth

3 oz. gin

1 orange slice, for garnish

Place the Campari, sweet vermouth, and gin in a mixing glass, fill the glass two-thirds of the way with ice, and stir until chilled and combined. Strain the cocktail into an Old Fashioned glass filled with ice or a chilled cocktail glass and garnish with the orange slice.

WHAT'S THE SECRET?

The canonical version of the drink is this drier rendition, which is better suited to the modern palate. But don't be afraid to experiment with the ratios, as the traditional preparation contained equal parts of the Campari, sweet vermouth, and gin. Just remain mindful that the herbal bite of the vermouth is there to build a bridge between the bittersweet Campari and the bold juniper kick of the gin. Don't hesitate to bounce back and forth between serving the cocktail up and on the rocks, as the changes in temperature will bring forth and mute different elements of the cocktail.

RIGHT THIS WAY

If the enchanting combination of vermouth and Campari in the Negroni has you wondering what other spirits can be lifted by the pair, know that others have been similarly inspired.

By switching the gin out for whiskey you end up with a Boulevardier, a drink that actually predates the Negroni. The nice thing about the Boulevardier is that, though traditionally made with bourbon, it is the rare cocktail that can accommodate whiskey in all its forms. The sweet, herbal bite of the vermouth is beautiful alongside a single-malt Scotch, while a spicy rye whiskey adds depth and a pleasant crispness to the proceedings.

SAZERAC

It is not easy to stand out in the sea of boozy concoctions that the carefree and celebratory culture of New Orleans has given birth to, but the Sazerac has managed to do just that. The drink was once so popular that when the United States outlawed the absinthe used in the traditional version, two New Orleans residents, J. Marion Legendre and Reginald Parker, created Herbsaint to ensure that the Sazerac could continue rolling along. Yes, it requires a little more finesse than most cocktails, but that just makes the final product all the more satisfying.

INGREDIENTS

¼ oz. Herbsaint
1 sugar cube
3 dashes of Peychaud's Bitters
1½ oz. rye whiskey
1 wide strip of lemon peel

Place the Herbsaint in a chilled Old Fashioned glass and swirl the glass until the inside is coated. Discard any excess Herbsaint. Place the sugar cube in a mixing glass, add the bitters, and muddle. Add the rye whiskey and a few ice cubes and stir until the cocktail is chilled and combined. Strain the cocktail into the prepared glass, express the strip of lemon peel over the cocktail, and then discard it.

WHAT'S THE SECRET?

Maintaining high standards with the rye whiskey. While you can get away with an inexpensive rye such as Old Overholt in an Old Fashioned, any cut corners will really stand out in the Sazerac, as there is no ice to cover up for even a slight step down. If the spicy punch of the rye alongside the anise-flavored Herbsaint is a bit too much for your taste, try replacing half of the rye with Cognac, which served as the cocktail's original base. The Cognac will add sweetness and smoothness, providing a soft bed for the rye to rest peacefully upon. Authorities are divided on whether adding the lemon peel to the drink after expressing its oils enhances or hampers the drink's intended effect, so try both approaches and see which you prefer.

RINSE AND REPEAT

The technique utilized with the Herbsaint in the Sazerac is known as "rinsing," and it is a great way to add another accent to a cocktail. Rinsing a glass with Cognac or a smoky, single-malt Scotch is a very simple and effective means of dressing up whiskey-based cocktails, and liqueurs can be used to put a twist on drinks featuring any spirit. Misting the inside of the glass with various spirits or tinctures is another way to add a subtle hint. To do this, simply fill a spray bottle with your desired accent, strain the cocktail into the glass, and generously mist the glass above the liquid.

WHITE RUSSIAN

As everyone knows, the Coen Brothers' late '90s masterwork, *The Big Lebowski*, breathed considerable life into this creamy cocktail, which had lost its way during the calorie-conscious '80s. By bringing this easy and delicious crowd-pleaser back into vogue, they just may have bought their unorthodox film—and the reluctant sage at the center of it—some of the considerable cachet they now carry.

INGREDIENTS

2 oz. vodka

1 oz. Kahlúa

Heavy cream, to taste

Place a few ice cubes in an Old Fashioned glass. Add the vodka and Kahlúa and stir until chilled. Top with a generous splash of heavy cream and slowly stir until combined.

WHAT'S THE SECRET?

While "The Dude" is laid back enough to tolerate powdered creamer and generic half-and-half in his "Caucasian," it pays to be a bit more discerning about the dairy component—no matter how big a fan of the movie you are. As you want a White Russian to feel as indulgent and rich as possible, heavy cream, with its minimum fat content of 36 percent, is essential. If heavy cream's thickness makes you wary, add just enough to lighten the drink slightly. Should you or a guest be one of those individuals who can't get enough coffee flavor, consider filling your ice-cube trays with room-temperaure coffee for cubes that will bolster the taste and prevent your drink from becoming too watery. Also, take your time composing this one, as the sight of the heavy cream purling in the glass is sure to set tongues wagging.

SANGRIA

Traditionally, the leathery, stone-fruit-centric flavor of Tempranillo or the spicy, red-fruit-forward Rioja are used, and even though *sangria* means "bleeding" in Spanish, any type of wine—red, white, rosé, or sparkling—can be employed to make a wonderful Sangria. This recipe hews closely to tradition, but a large part of Sangria's charm is its adaptability. So long as wine, fruit, booze, and bubbles are arranged in this agreeable ratio, you can be confident that the result is going to be delicious.

INGREDIENTS

1 (750 ml) bottle of dry red wine

2 oranges, sliced into thin half-moons

2 Granny Smith apples,
cored, seeded, and chopped

2 cups seedless grapes

2 oz. brandy

1 cup plain or citrus-flavored seltzer

Place all of the ingredients, except for the seltzer, in a large pitcher or container and stir to combine. Cover and refrigerate for at least 4 hours, though longer is strongly recommended. When ready to serve, add ice and the seltzer and gently stir until chilled.

WHAT'S THE SECRET?

Using fruit that complements the spirit you choose to fortify the Sangria with is an easy way to produce a pleasant, flavorful punch. Here, the seedless grapes and the brandy—which is the result of distilling wine—accomplish this charge. But you could also choose to play off the oranges and swap the brandy out for triple sec, Cointreau, or Grand Marnier. Also, don't go overboard when purchasing the wine. You don't want something cheap, but always operate with the knowledge that the wine is a backdrop in Sangria, rather than the centerpiece. A dry, fruity red from the Mediterranean or one of the crisp whites that New Zealand has become renowned for are good standbys when assembling ingredients.

GIVE THE PEOPLE WHAT THEY WANT

Sangria is not the only beverage that should be presented in a pitcher. In fact, if you get enough people on board, you can make a large batch of any cocktail, so long as you remain mindful of the ratio that produces the desired results on a small scale, and add enough ice to properly chill and dilute the cocktail. To double-check that it's safe to proceed, make yourself a small drink using the decided-upon proportions before whipping up the entire batch. Trust me, there's nothing worse than dumping half a bottle of good gin into a pitcher only to find out that the tonic water's gone flat in the refrigerator. Should you end up frequently serving people with similar tastes, it might be worth investing in a large pitcher with a lipped spout. This will make it much easier to keep the ice and fruit in the pitcher from making its way into a drink when you're pouring.

THE FINISHING
TOUCH

YOU CAN CALL IT a day after mixing a cocktail and straining it into a glass, but a drink isn't truly complete until the garnish has been added. Able to provide a burst of color as well as an aroma and flavor that ties the entire package together, knowing how to finish strong is the final piece of the mixology puzzle.

While the cocktail world, particularly those drinks that reside in the realm of tiki, is home to increasingly fabulous garnishes, there's no need for you to fashion dolphins out of bananas or soak a slice of lime in overproof rum so that it can be set alight in the glass. Simply knowing how to cut a citrus peel so that you get all of the bright zest and none of the bitter pith, or how to affix a lime wedge on the glass's rim so a guest can easily squeeze its juice into their drink is enough to seal the deal. When done correctly, the garnish gilds the lily—adding an aesthetic component that transforms the process of crafting cocktails into theater, and an accent that helps the other elements shine.

In order to transform citrus into satisfactory

garnishes, always wash and dry the fruit thoroughly before starting to work with it. And to ensure that they do not become dried out, try to make citrus-based garnishes as close to cocktail hour as possible.

Beyond that, a few tools and some practice are required. Common kitchen workhorses like the paring knife, vegetable peeler, box grater, and microplane will serve you well. But if you want to take things a step further, these specialized tools can clear the way:

Channel Knife: The U-shaped blade of this classic bar tool is essential if you're looking to create long and swanky strips of zest.

Pronged Tip Bar Knife: The long, thin handle makes elaborate cuts a cinch, while the tip makes it easy to spear cherries and olives.

"Y" Garnish Peeler: This professional piece of kit bears close resemblance to a safety razor, and the "Y" stands for "yes" in terms of pulling off whatever duty it is charged with.

To create a typical strip of citrus zest, place a just-sharpened paring knife between the zest and white pith and twist the fruit, while applying moderate pressure, until you have removed the required amount of zest. For cocktails that require a wider strip of zest, such as a Sazerac, employ the same method but use a vegetable peeler. The resulting strip can then be held above the cocktail and twisted into a tight spiral to express the aromatic oils into the drink. Once you've done that, either discard the twist or drop it into a drink to add a burst of color and a touch of refinement.

Turning zest into a twist

While the twist requires the most finesse and technique of the citrus garnishes, the others do need a bit of care if you want to get them right. To cut a proper wedge of citrus, slice a ¼" off each end of a citrus fruit. Next, cut the fruit in half, lengthwise, and set one of the halves, cut-side down, on your cutting board. Finally, slice it at an angle, lengthwise, and you should have a perfect little wedge. Cut a slit in the midsection of the wedge so that it can rest on the rim of a glass.

Creating a citrus wedge

For a citrus wheel, cut the fruit in half crosswise and then make a parallel cut about ⅛" to ¼" above the initial cut. Cut the wheel from the edge to the center so that it can rest on the glass's rim.

Fashioning a citrus wheel

Using herbs such as sprigs of mint, rosemary, or thyme as a garnish requires nothing more than your hands. Since you are utilizing an herb for its aroma as much as anything, lay the sprigs or leaves in the palm of one hand and give them a good smack with the other before placing them in the cocktail. This bit of sternness will whip an herb into shape, activating its essential oils.

When garnishing a cocktail with olives, it is traditional to place three on a skewer. One is consumed following the first sip, and the remaining two after the last. If that seems like too many, simply drop one into the cocktail. Olives can also be stuffed with various ingredients to add another layer of flavor. While the sweet pimento remains the most common by far, garlic cloves, almonds, blue cheese, jalapeño peppers, and even anchovies have become frequent fillings for olives.

And, finally, if a cocktail calls for a maraschino cherry, steer clear of the ruby red version that the supermarket has accustomed you to. That chemically saturated, super-sweet variety can't hold a candle to the true maraschino king: Luxardo. Made from the sour marasca cherries that only grow in the sandy soils of Croatia's Dalmatian mountain range, they are preserved in a syrup consisting only of sugar and the marasca's juice. A Luxardo cherry has a deep-red, almost-purple color that lends a touch of class to a Manhattan, as well as a rich flavor that carries notes of almond. They are far more expensive than the syrupy charlatan, but worth every penny if you are serious about making the best cocktails you can.

FURTHER READING

Jim Meehan
Meehan's Bartender Manual
Arguably the most comprehensive bartending
guide out there, written by one of the individuals
who keyed the cocktail renaissance.

Dave Arnold
Liquid Intelligence
A fun book that goes from the basics of cocktail
making all the way to molecular gastronomic
techniques. A helpful resource once you've got a
solid foundation and are ready to try your hand
at mixology.

Dale DeGroff
The Craft of the Cocktail
A New York legend takes you on a tour through
the classic cocktails he built his reputation upon.
The book that introduced myself, and countless
others, to the art of cocktail making.

Jeffrey Morgenthaler
The Bar Book
By breaking down ingredients and proper technique, this book will provide you with the fundamentals so that you won't miss the mark when you're ready to get creative.

Kingsley Amis
On Drink
Helpful tips and valuable perspective provided by one of England's best-known authors and carousers.

David Kaplan & Nick Fauchald
Death & Co: Modern Classic Cocktails
One of the most influential bars to come out of the craft cocktail scene, this book features incredibly creative drinks, as well as guidance on buying and using spirits, mind-set, and technique.

GLOSSARY

While this book will provide you with everything you need to feel confident getting started, you will no doubt encounter things you don't recognize once you venture out of its cozy confines. Here's a collection of some common terms that you might come across, plus some further elaboration on material contained within.

Apéritif: A drink that stimulates the appetite. Examples of apéritifs are Campari, Suze and soda, any Champagne-based cocktail, and Lillet.

Brut: An appellation given to the driest sparkling wine. It is occasionally broken down further into "extra brut" and "brut natural," with the latter indicating that no sugar has been added.

Cordial: A sweet substance made from fruit or flowers that is added to a cocktail or consumed by itself. While cordials are thought of as alcoholic in the US, they are typically nonalcoholic in other countries.

Crème: Refers not to the presence of cream, but to a liqueur with a large amount of sugar added, to the point where it acquires a nearly syrup-like consistency.

Dash: A quick addition, usually of a liquid ingredient. It is roughly equivalent to 1 teaspoon, but not an exact measurement.

Digestif: A drink that helps you digest your meal. Examples are Fernet-Branca and drinks made with brandy, Chartreuse, or Sherry.

Float: A technique where a small amount of alcohol is layered on top of a cocktail. Alcohol that is floated should be poured very slowly, an effect a number of bartenders achieve by pouring the liquid over the back of a barspoon.

Fortified wine: A wine to which a distilled spirit, usually brandy, has been added in order preserve and flavor it.

Liqueur: A combination of a distilled spirit and a flavorful element that is typically sweet. Usually very strong in flavor, a liqueur is primarily used to provide an accent in cocktails, rather than consumed on its own. Popular examples are crème de menthe, Kahlúa, Grand Marnier, and Midori.

Overproof: Refers to a spirit that is more than 50 percent ethanol when it is bottled.

Part: The suggested ratio of a particular component in a cocktail recipe. Allows the recipe to be easily adapted to different kinds of glassware and serving sizes.

Pinch: A small amount of material that can be picked up and held between two fingers. Roughly equivalent to 1/16 of a teaspoon, though not an exact measure.

Rim: Dipping the wet rim of a glass into a salt, sugar, or a seasoning blend before pouring the cocktail into it. Used to accent cocktails without affecting the balance of flavors in what is being mixed.

Sherry: A fortified wine that is made from white grapes that are grown in Andalusia, a territory in southern Spain. After the wine has been fortified, it is stored in casks of North American oak.

Sloe gin: A sweet, red liqueur that is the result of steeping sloe drupes, a relative of the plum, in gin.

Spent: Refers to a piece of citrus, fruit, or vegetable that the juice has been removed from.

Splash: A quick addition, usually of a liquid ingredient. Larger than a dash, it is roughly equivalent to 1 tablespoon, but not an exact measurement.

Tincture: A typically alcoholic extract of plant or animal material. Produced by steeping an element in a solvent such as alcohol or vinegar for 2 to 3 weeks.

Top: To fill the remainder of a glass with a particular ingredient, most commonly utilized when adding something that is carbonated, like sparkling wine or seltzer water.

ABOUT THE AUTHOR

Kurt Maitland started his spirits journey with drams of Jameson in college, and has been exploring the world of spirits in general, and whiskey in particular, ever since. He lives in New York City and is the deputy editor of the popular The Whiskey Reviewer website, the curator of the Manhattan Whiskey Club, and the owner of Whiskey Selections. He is also the author of *Drink: The Ultimate Cocktail Book.*

DISTILLED IDEAS
FOR CURIOUS MINDS

Curated to be useful, entertaining, and informative, Curios range from cultural appraisals to culinary guides, packing plenty of punch no matter the subject.

FORTHCOMING

ABOUT CIDER MILL PRESS BOOK PUBLISHERS

Good ideas ripen with time. From seed to harvest, Cider Mill Press brings fine reading, information, and entertainment together between the covers of its creatively crafted books. Our Cider Mill bears fruit twice a year, publishing a new crop of titles each spring and fall.

"Where Good Books Are Ready for Press"

Visit us online at
www.cidermillpress.com
or write to us at
PO Box 454
12 Spring St.
Kennebunkport, Maine 04046